THE LITTLE BOOK OF
MOON MAGIC
FRANCIS NIGHTINGALE

Red Wheel

THE LITTLE BOOK OF MOON MAGIC

This edition first published in 2024 by Red Wheel, an imprint of
Red Wheel/Weiser, LLC
With offices at:
65 Parker Street, Suite 7
Newburyport, MA 01950
www.redwheelweiser.com

Copyright © Octopus Publishing Group Limited, 2024

ISBN: 978-1-59003-556-6

Printed and bound in China
1010 Printing International Ltd

10 9 8 7 6 5 4 3 2 1

The spells and rituals in this book are for information only and should not be
practiced by anyone without proper training. Readers using the information in
this book do so entirely at their own risk, and the author and publisher accept
no liability if adverse effects are caused.

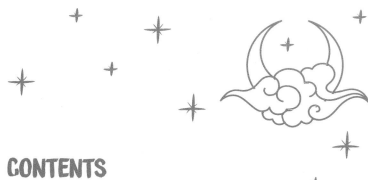

CONTENTS

INTRODUCTION

Because it is always there in the night sky, it is easy to forget what a strange, beautiful, and wonderful thing the moon is. For many of us it is only when we find ourselves caught off guard—by a moon that glows redder than usual, or hangs lower in the sky, is bigger, smaller, or cut exactly in half like a ripe piece of fruit— that we find ourselves consumed by wonder.

Moon magic explores this most fascinating of objects, which is as captivating to scientists as it is to the casters of spells, as enthralling to astrologers as it is to poets and dreamers, and as spellbinding to those who tell us tales as to those who just lie back and gaze at it.

To the ancient Greeks, it was "Selene," to the Romans, "Luna." We know that people at the dawn of time worshipped it, and those of our own time have been drawn to walk on it, which is still humanity's biggest step. We all know the moon moves the tides, but few of us know it moves and shapes the Earth's surface too.

We also know it moves and shapes us too—changing our moods, sometimes keeping us awake and sometimes helping us sleep. Across the world and across time humans have sought solace in the moon, have told stories about it and sought its favor.

The Little Book of Moon Magic will take you on a journey: you will learn facts about the moon, but also stories about it from all around the world. You will also learn spells to perform during different phases of the moon, such as spells for catharsis, manifesting and love. And you will learn to meditate with the moon, to find an inner peace and grow your psychic energy.

It will still catch you off guard sometimes, though! It's the moon's way.

CHAPTER ONE

PHASES OF THE MOON

One of the most delightful things about the moon is it never seems to be the same two nights in a row. It seems to come closer, move away, drop in during the day, and then hide as a tiny sliver in the night.

The phases of the moon, from a new moon to a full moon and back again, have been eulogized in song, studied by astrologers and gardeners, and can provoke wonder in the youngest child and the oldest sage.

In this chapter, we will look in detail at all these phases and the associations attached to each one. We will look at how these phases change throughout the year, and what it means for life on Earth.

But first, what is the moon anyway? What is it doing up there?

WHAT IS THE MOON MADE OF?

Spoiler alert: it's not cheese! The moon is actually made of oxygen, silicon, magnesium, iron, calcium, and aluminium, plus small amounts of other elements. To put it more briefly, it is mostly rocks. But these rocks are in all sorts of wonderful and uncanny formations, such as dead volcanoes, impact craters, and lava flows.

In fact, early scientists thought these lava flows that form dark patches on the moon's surface were actually seas. They called them "mares," which is Latin for sea. This means the dark patches on the moon have names such as "The Sea of Clouds," "The Sea of Vapors," "The Sea of Cleverness," and "The Sea of Tranquility," the last of which being the first location on another celestial body to be visited by humans.

It may be tranquil now, but no human would have wanted to be standing there when it was created by exploding volcanoes 4.533 billion years ago.

THE FORMATION OF THE MOON

What happened 4.533 billion years ago? According to Finnish mythology, Ilmatar, the daughter of the air, allowed a duck to lay its eggs on her knee. The eggs fell, and the whites became the moon and the yolks became the sun. It is not known what happened to the duck.

Nowadays, it is thought that our Earth was crashed into by another planet, roughly the size of Mars. The colliding planet is sometimes called Theia, named after the mythical Greek Titan who was the mother of Selene, the goddess of the moon.

The collision sent large pieces of both Earth and Theia flying into space, where they were stirred together like in a mixing bowl and became the moon.

So, for the last 4.533 billion years the Earth and moon have continued their celestial dance around each other. As for what happened to Theia—unfortunately, like the duck, no one is really quite sure.

THE PHASES OF THE MOON

Generally, we talk about four major phases of the moon: the new moon, the first quarter, the full moon, and the final quarter. The moon waxes—gets bigger—from the start of the new moon up to becoming a full moon, and then wanes—gets smaller—from the full moon to the next new moon. This takes about 29.5 days—a lunar month.

If we want to be more precise, we can even say that there are eight phases, four primary and four intermediate: new moon, waxing crescent, first quarter, waxing gibbous, full moon, waning gibbous, final quarter, waning crescent.

Our calendar is an attempt to approximate the phases of the moon. The fact that most calendars in history have tied themselves to the moon in one way or another just goes to show how important the moon is.

HOW DO THE PHASES OF THE MOON HAPPEN?

Back in ancient Greece, it was widely believed that the moon was in fact flat. The belief was that one side of the moon was silvery-white, while the other side was black, and it was the orbiting of this half-white, half-black moon around the Earth that caused the lunar phases. Champions of this idea included the philosopher Aristotle.

This itself was seen as a radical new theory—many of the general population still believed that the moon was being driven across the sky in a chariot by the goddess Selene, and the different phases were different paths she would take. Some even believed the moon was a deity itself—after all, the sun was.

Undoubtably there were some ferocious debates between those who thought the moon was flat and the "fans of Selene," but they were nothing compared to the theory that another Greek philosopher Anaxagoras was about to unleash.

WHY THE MOON IS LIGHT

We don't know much about Anaxagoras. He was a foreigner in Greece and tried to give scientific explanations of meteor eclipses, rainbows, and the sun (which he thought was a ball of burning metal).

It was Anaxagoras who first proposed that the light of the moon was reflected off the sun. "It is the sun that puts brightness into the moon," he wrote. This view was not popular with either those who thought the moon was flat or the "fans of Selene," nor with the most famous Greek philosopher, Plato, who thought the moon was not only illuminated, but also a god. Current science sides with Anaxagoras—the phases of the moon are related to where the sun, Earth and moon are aligned.

Both Plato and Anaxagoras now have craters on the moon named after them—but Anaxagoras was sentenced to death for his beliefs; he avoided this penalty by going into exile.

Of course, the truth about the phases of the moon is that science can only explain so much. Throughout history and throughout the world, individual and whole societies have felt the effects of the phases of the moon on their emotions, their health, and the way they sleep and eat.

A lot of ancient cultures, and quite a few contemporary ones, would be astonished at how many of us have lost touch with our natural connection with the moon. Anaxagoras might have worked out that the moon gave no light of its own, but he also believed that it had a unique connection to human beings.

Some believe that this lost connection with the moon has made us all much less open to the world. It's up to each of us to give ourselves back over to the influence of our nearest neighbor in the sky, and to realize the pleasures and opportunities that affords us, starting with each of the phases.

Shoot for the moon —
even if you miss it,
you will land
among the stars.

Anonymous

THE NEW MOON

In technical terms, a new moon is when the sun and the moon have the same "ecliptic longitude"—but put simply it's when the Earth gets between the sun and the moon, so the whole thing is in shadow.

It has always been worshipped as a phase of new beginnings and a time of introspection. Just as the moon appears to become a small crescent but contains within it the full moon that will soon burst forth, so too can those who are open to its influence take time for withdrawal and contemplation.

Some people take a moment at the time of the new moon to set down their goals and intentions. By doing this we can watch our projects follow the course of the lunar phase—there is nothing more rewarding than achieving a goal to the rhythm of the moon.

NEW MOON,
NEW PROJECTS, NEW YOU

Those who work the land have known about the power of the new moon since time began. It is a perfect time to plant any flowers and vegetables that grow above the ground. As the moon begins waxing to fullness, these crops will be encouraged to draw the growing light into themselves and grow in harmony with their celestial mother.

This is why the time of the new moon is the best time to start new projects. As the plants grow to greet the full moon, we can clear a space for ourselves to start some of those endeavors where we need something more than our own power to carry us forward.

By aligning ourselves with the waxing moon we borrow some of its power—it won't mind; it has plenty to share! So, when the moon is just a tiny sliver, remember, it is ready to grow along with your plans.

NEW MOON "SUPERSTITIONS"

Since time immemorial, the influence of the moon has been understood. Some people might call these superstitions, but who's to say that this ancient wisdom isn't true?

If you do see a new moon and you have change in your pocket, be sure to move it from where it is. This will make sure that your riches increase with the waxing of the moon. If you don't move the money, you will end this phase of the moon poorer than you started.

Also, according to the *Farmer's Almanac*, try not to view the new moon for the first time through a window. You'll break a dish soon after. Of course, farmer's work outside most of the time, so it is easier—but the wisest farmer always makes sure they have a dish of no value perched on their windowsill, so they can let it topple if they are caught out.

WAXING CRESCENT

If you've planted your flowers and crops, filled out your journal, and started new projects, the waxing crescent moon is a time of consolidation and activity. Hopefully some of your projects will flower early! But just as the moon grows slowly and steadily, allow your personal journey to grow organically.

The Inuit people of Greenland believe that there was a family quarrel between the sibling deities Annigan and Malina. Malina stormed off, and her brother Annigan went in pursuit. So dedicated is he to the task that he forgets to eat, which is why the moon wanes. The waxing moon shows that he has found her and begun to eat again.

But some have proposed we be more like Annigan when we eat during this time of the month. The new moon is a time to give our stomachs a rest, and then gradually build up our food intake as the belly of the moon grows full.

FIRST QUARTER MOON

Is there a more stunning moon that the first quarter moon? When it is perfect, the moon seems cut in half, a straight line from top to bottom. Three quarters of the moon is hidden from us, hence why this phase is called the first quarter moon.

The quarter of the moon that you can see depends on where on the Earth you are. In the northern hemisphere the right side is lit up, in the southern it is the left. And while we think of the moon as a night-time object, in fact the first quarter moon rises at about midday and sets at midnight. Of course, all of the stars are there all day too, we just can't see them!

FIRST QUARTER PHASE— DEEPEST WISHES

As is well known, the first quarter moon is an ideal time for reflection on where you are heading and how much you are beginning to bloom.

But it is also a time for deeper reflection. It can be all too easy to stay on the surface of our desires when we should dig a little deeper. What are your deepest wishes? It is time to think of them. This is for you and you only—although perhaps you can tell them to the moon too. By saying these things out loud, we can start to manifest them as real things.

It is also a time to think about what might be standing in the way of those desires. Sometimes it's other people, sometimes it's you. The moon will respect your honesty and help you on your path.

THE JEWELED SCIMITAR

If you are lucky, two days after the first quarter moon you can observe one of the most beautiful images the eye can feast on. Known as "The Jeweled Scimitar" or "The Golden Handle," the sun briefly lights up the 260-kilometer-long Montes Jura mountain range, while the Sinus Iridum ("Bay of Rainbows") below it remains dark.

This gives the impression of a curved "handle" near what is called the "terminator" of the quarter moon, meaning the line down its middle, separating light and dark. You won't always be able to see it, because sometimes it occurs when the moon is below your horizon, but when you do you will be bewitched by its beauty. It can last anything up to a few hours and is truly magical because of it.

As for the Bay of Rainbows, there is no "bay" of course, let alone rainbows. It was named in 1651 by the Italian astronomer Giovanni Battista Riccioli, who located it next to the "Sea of Storms"!

WAXING GIBBOUS

The moon has captured the imagination of wordsmiths for millennia, and the phase of the moon that is most loved by those who love language is the waxing gibbous. The word "gibbous" comes from the Latin *gibbus*, which means "humped" (like a camel's back) or more poetically "protuberant."

It was first used to describe this phase of the moon in 1690, which is a pity as Shakespeare would have adored the word. A famous lover of words and moons, he was long gone by 1690 but Romeo's "O, swear not by the moon, th' inconstant moon / That monthly changes in her circle orb" could have been much improved by adding gibbous.

Fortunately, Shakespeare was around for "waxing" (which means to grow, be fruitful, increase, become powerful, flourish) and "waning" (to make or become smaller gradually, diminish, decline, fade), and in *Henry VI*, he writes "I seek not to wax great by others' waning," which remains a good way to live even now.

FOLLOWING THE MOON'S LEAD

Like the first quarter moon, the waxing gibbous moon often appears in the daytime, rising in the east as the sun sets in the west. In technical terms, any time between the light hitting 50.1 percent and 99.9 percent of the moon is a gibbous phase, although the naked eye can be excused for being a percent or two out!

This is a time to look at your goals and see if you are on track to achieve them by the full moon. Of course, in a perfect world any goal could be reached in the two weeks but as we all know this is not always possible.

Therefore, it is time to follow the moon's lead again—as it changes, you too can change and reevaluate your plans. It is also a good time to look for synchronicity—the moon will often be trying to tell you things at this point, so look out for patterns in the world and in your plans.

THE FULL MOON

And suddenly, at the end of the lunar cycle, there it is: the spectacular full moon.

If you haven't been observing the phases, then it still comes as a surprise—on a clear night it can seem almost like day, although a day suffused in blue or yellow light. The Earth and moon in perfect alignment with the sun.

There is a technical name for this that is almost as fun to say as "gibbous"—it is called "syzygy." Unlike the other phases of the moon, it can only ever appear at night as the Earth stands directly between the sun and the moon, so the moon must be on the dark side of the Earth.

Sometimes a full moon can seem to last more than one night, but don't be fooled—to the naked eye a moon 98 percent lit up seems full.

SUPERMOON AND MICROMOON

As anyone who has gazed at the night sky will tell you, sometimes the full moon is huge, sometimes it is much smaller. The biggest moon is called a supermoon and the smallest moon is called a micromoon.

This is nothing to do with anything expanding or contracting. It is simply that the moon does not move around the Earth in a circle, but in an ellipse.

When the moon is at the far ends of the ellipse it looks (and is!) further away, and when it is at the middle of the ellipse it is closer. That is why the moon changes size, most strikingly during its full phase.

Its closest proximity is called its perigee and its most distant is its apogee. One big effect of the perigee moon is that the tides are higher and lower—the gravitational pull of the moon is added to that of the sun, so the water moves more. At the apogee it moves less.

SPECIAL TYPES OF FULL MOON

You've no doubt heard the expression "Once in a blue moon..." meaning something that happens very rarely. According to NASA, a blue moon is the second full moon in a month, and it actually occurs once every two to three years.

The reason for this is simple—as we know, the actual time it takes for a lunar cycle is 29.5 days, and our calendars generally have 30 or 31 days in one month. Which means some years there will be a thirteenth full moon—one of the months must double up.

This also means that February, having only 28 days, never has a blue moon, and sometimes even has no full moon at all. This is known as a Black Moon month.

Sometimes a blue moon coincides with a supermoon—a super blue moon. The next isn't until January 2037, but don't worry if you miss that one— there will be another super blue moon in March of that same year!

While a blue moon isn't blue, a blood moon is definitely red. It occurs during a lunar eclipse when the Earth is perfectly in line between the sun and the moon. It blocks the sun's rays, and the only light that reaches the moon's surface is from the edges of the Earth's atmosphere. The blue light is scattered by the air molecules from Earth's atmosphere, leaving only the red.

A less malevolent moon is the harvest moon, the light bright moon that appears close to the horizon at the start of autumn around the time of the equinox. Before there was electric lighting, and still now in deeply rural places, farmers depended on the moon's light to bring in the last of the harvest. Even now there are harvest moon festivals around the world—if you want to visit the country and enjoy a feast, try to arrive in early autumn!

FULL MOON FORGIVENESS

It goes without saying that humans have always venerated and sometimes feared the full moon. Whole religions have been built on it, and it is obviously hard to explain the existence of werewolves without its transformative powers!

If you've been planning your life around the phases of the moon, the full moon should be a time of celebration and reflection. If some of your goals haven't come to fruition, don't worry—the phases of the moon come round again and again, and you will no doubt have moved things forward.

It is also a time of release, to let go of burdens, to forgive yourself, and to forgive others. When we reflect on the fact that in thousands of years the full moon will still be shining down on us, our problems suddenly seem a lot less significant. Use its light to illuminate the world around you and see what is really important.

WANING GIBBOUS

And after the full moon comes the waning. The Japanese writer Ai Yazawa reminds us that the waning of the moon is only a matter of perspective: "But even when the moon looks like it's waning... it's actually never changing shape. Don't ever forget that." From where we stand the waning gibbous moon is just as beautiful as the waxing one, perhaps even more beautiful because it carries a note of melancholy as we move away from the full moon.

It is also the true moon of harvest and the Greeks associated the waning gibbous with Demeter, goddess of agriculture.

Like the waxing gibbous, it can appear during the day, because it has risen later in the evening, well after sunset. If you are out late and you see a moon begin to rise well after sunset, chances are it's a waning gibbous, and you'll be seeing it in the morning too (depending on how late you are up!).

A TIME OF GRATITUDE

The waning gibbous moon is a time where one can withdraw a little into oneself, and do so in gentle stages. Too often in our lives we can feel overwhelmed by too much sound and light, and deny ourselves the pleasure of stepping back and looking inside ourselves, or just around to those nearest and dearest.

The waning gibbous should be a time of reflection and gratitude—we should be grateful to the people around us who love and support us, and grateful to ourselves for the things we have achieved. These might be small things or big things, but they are equally important.

After all, the moon has performed a big act in moving from its new to full phase, and yet this is also a small undertaking, as all it has to do is go with the flow. That doesn't make what it does any less astonishing.

FINAL QUARTER

Also known as the third quarter, the final quarter forms a perfect symmetry with the first, as the other quarter of the moon is illuminated, darkness covering the rest. Rising at midnight and setting at noon, like the first quarter it produces the smallest tides, as the sun and the moon pull in different directions. These are known as neap tides, as opposed to the king tides of the full moon.

This pulling in different directions can affect us too. Just as the two heavenly bodies pull in different directions, sometimes this phase of the moon can cause us to feel a little on edge. It is then that we need to seek clarity and light.

Don't forget that this interplay is as natural to us as when the sun and moon are in alignment. We should not try to fight it, but accept the tumult and learn from it. After all, it's just a phase!

WANING CRESCENT

The poet T. S. Eliot wrote that in his end was his beginning, and in his beginning was his end. So it is for the moon. As it wanes it returns to the crescent shape that followed the new moon, and this time it is the other side of it that appears sickle shaped.

It is often visible in the predawn, and when it is it usually has with it a companion star—Venus. These are the two brightest objects in the night sky, the warm light of the moon contrasting with the solid light of the planet. At this hour Venus blazes with 15 times the light of the nearest star, Sirius.

The moon and the planet are caught in an eternal dance; sometimes the crescent turns its back on Venus, sometimes it seems to cradle it. They have been locked together for all time, bringing wonder.

THE DA VINCI GLOW

Have you ever noticed when there is a crescent moon near the horizon, you can actually see the rest of the moon in outline? This is known as either "earthshine" or as the "Da Vinci glow," named after the famous artist Leonardo da Vinci. It was da Vinci who first looked to explain what many had called "the old moon in the new moon's arms" (or vice versa).

Even though da Vinci lived before Copernicus worked out that the Earth went around the sun, rather than the sun going around the Earth, da Vinci was still able to work out that the ghostly glow came from the Earth, not the sun.

He was wrong about one thing though: he thought the reflection came off the oceans, but it is in fact the clouds that reflect the light. As a result, it is best seen where the sky is clear but where there are enough clouds elsewhere to throw the light upwards. It is a rare and beautiful thing to see.

CLEARING AWAY THE CLUTTER

And so the moon has completed its monthly journey. The waning crescent gives birth to the new moon, and for those who connect with its phases it is a time to think about the previous month and clear the decks in anticipation of the new one.

Some people find this is a good time to clear away the clutter of their lives. Some of this is physical—the waning crescent moon can be a time to clean the house or clean your desk. That way you can welcome the new moon into a space in which both of you can thrive.

But it is also a time to clear the mental clutter. Take a warm bath, light some candles, and reflect on the previous month. If the things that have pulled you in different directions have left you misaligned, now is the time to bring them back into correspondence.

As you greet the new moon and wonder at its future journey, let the moon greet a new you and wonder about yours.

With freedom, books, flowers, and the moon, who could not be happy?

OSCAR WILDE

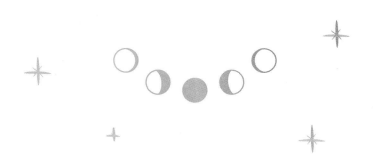

CHAPTER TWO

MOON LORE

The moon is the closest heavenly body to Earth, and our most intimate neighbor. Of all the celestial bodies it is the most subject to change, to changes of position and changes of form.

Is it any wonder that since the dawn of time it has inspired more myths and legends than any other object?

To our first ancestors it must have appeared as a baffling visitation, an object of veneration and fear. To the scientists and astrologers, it is no less mysterious, and every new piece of understanding brings more questions. Where we had myths, we now have scientific theories, but even once we explain every inch of our lunar neighbor, her mysterious hold on us will remain inexplicable and mystic.

To travel through the stories and myths of the moon is to travel through the stories and myths of human existence, and to learn its lessons is to learn the lessons of what it is to be human.

CHANG'E AND THE ELIXIR OF IMMORTALITY

Once upon a time there was not just one sun in the sky, but ten, scorching the Earth. Hou Yi, also known as the "Lord Archer" in China, took his bow and arrow and shot down nine of the suns. He was rewarded with two vessels of the Elixir of Immortality, one for him and one for his wife, the beautiful Chang'e.

The next day, as he was out hunting, his apprentice, Fengmeng, jealous of his master's skill and wanting to become immortal himself, broke into Hou Yi's house to try to steal the elixir. He encountered Chang'e who, rather than give up the elixir to the evil Fengmeng, drank both portions herself. Then she flew upward to the moon with her pet rabbit Yu Tu, where she took up residence to stay close to her husband.

There she lives to this day, a symbol of nostalgia and solitude, and the subject of hundreds of poems, myths, and legends.

THIRTEEN NOTCHES

An artwork was carved approximately 25,000 years ago, in what we now call France. Known as the Venus of Laussel, this 18-inch limestone carving of a voluptuous woman holding a horn in one upraised hand is believed to give us clues as to how our Paleolithic ancestors measured time.

For a long time, the association between the phases of the moon and fertility has been a staple of moon lore. The lunar month and the menstrual cycle having nearly identical durations has led humans throughout time and across the world to speculate on the moon's influence on procreation.

The horn that the Venus of Laussel holds has 13 notches, and archaeologists believe that the notches are symbols of the number of moons in the year, or the number of menstrual cycles, or both. Many cave paintings from the region also seem to contain 13 marks, notches, or figures. Could it be that these societies planned their pregnancies around the phases of the moon?

THOTH AND THE
FIVE EXTRA DAYS

To see how important the moon was to the Ancient Egyptians we need look no further than to their god of the moon, Thoth. As the Egyptians organized more of their life around the lunar cycles, Thoth took on more and more attributes—he became the god not only of the moon, but of measurement, time, magic, science, art, and writing, which he is said to have invented.

It is said that he also invented the 365-day year. Before that the year was 360 days long, but the goddess of the sky and stars, Nut, was infertile during those days. Thoth gambled with the moon for 1/72nd of its light to make five fertile days.

Thoth won, and Nut gave birth to three sons: Osiris, Horus, and Set; and two daughters Isis and Nephthys—some of the great deities of Egypt. The moon has never been given that light back, and so we still have 365-day years.

BRIGHTLY
TRESSED GODDESS

As we have seen, the ancient Greeks revered Selene as the goddess of the moon and she was also its personification. Her name means "light, brightness, gleam." In early accounts she is noted for being "brightly tressed," her hair as golden as the light of the moon. Later, like the moon, she has horns, but these do not detract from her beauty.

Selene's father was the sun god Hyperion. As her brother Helios drives the sun across the heavens in a chariot, so Selene drives the moon. Helios has four horses, Selene only two, as the moon is more delicate. Only the witches of Thessaly can stop her nightly journeys, and what we call lunar eclipses are them working their magic. But Selene always recovers and continues her course.

Known for her love affairs, Selene is also the goddess of childbirth, which is why there is the belief that it is less painful to give birth during a full moon. Isn't it?

WOLVES! WOLVES!

In Norse mythology, which was believed in northern Germany and Scandinavia, the moon is not the sister of the sun, but his brother. His name is Máni, meaning "moon," and he and his brother Sól must pass across the sky each day to help humans count the years. In fact, the Norse elves called Máni "the counter of years" and it is believed that Norse calendars relied on the moon more than the sun.

As we know, both the sun and moon don't move along the same path every day, and this may be because both Sól and Máni have a long-running dispute with a pair of wolves called Skoll and Hati, who chase them across the skies trying to eat them. Should they succeed, the world will end, so let's hope the brothers never get tired.

Some think that Máni might be the origin of one of the great lunar myths—the myth of the Man in the Moon.

THE MAN IN THE MOON

We've all seen the "Man in the Moon" even if we have to squint, upside down in the southern hemisphere, the right way up in the northern.

To science it is simply an effect called "pareidolia"—humans seeing a meaningful image in a random visual pattern, like seeing faces in toast or clouds that take on recognizable shapes.

We do this when we look at the mountains and the seas of the moon.

However, a more interesting account comes from Latvia. According to legend, it is not a face we see but another part of the anatomy. One day two women were collecting water naked. One remarked to the other how beautiful the moon is. The other, jealous, said even her bottom was prettier than the moon, and proceeded to "moon the moon." As punishment the moon goddess Dievs imprisoned her on the moon, with her bottom forever exposed.

THE RABBIT
IN THE MOON

In both East Indian and Indigenous American folklore, there is no Man in the Moon (nor the nether parts of a Latvian woman). Instead, there is a rabbit, much like the companion of China's Chang'e, who is continually pounding the Elixir of Immortality with a mortar and pestle.

The Buddhist Jataka stories tell of a monkey, an otter, a jackal, and a rabbit who resolved to do an act of kindness the next full moon. A hungry old man begged them for food. The monkey gathered nuts for him, the otter brought him fish, and the jackal brought him a lizard. Having no hunting skills, the rabbit threw itself onto the old man's fire, sacrificing its own life to feed the man.

The man then revealed himself to be Śakra, ruler of the heavens. He brought the rabbit back to life and then carved its image in the moon as a reminder to all people that charity is the greatest of all virtues.

The belief that a rabbit can be seen in the moon is shared by several Indigenous American stories. In one Aztec myth, the humble Nanahuatzin sacrificed himself in a fire to become the new sun, but the wealthy and boastful Tēcciztēcatl hesitated four times before becoming the moon. Due to his cowardice, the god decided he should not shine as brightly as the sun, and so threw a rabbit in his face to diminish the light.

The Cree nation tells of a rabbit who wished to go to the moon and for all the birds to take him there. All refused except a crane. The rabbit held onto his legs all the way, which stretched them and left them elongated, as all cranes are to this day. When they arrived the rabbit's paws were bloodied from holding on, and when he touched the head of the crane to say thank you, he left the red mark that cranes carry even now.

MERLPAL MARI PATHANU

In most Indigenous Australian cultures, unlike many other places on Earth, the sun is female and the moon is male. To the Yolngu people, he was once a thin and handsome man, as when the moon is a crescent, but over time he grew fat and lazy, until becoming completely full in his belly. Angered by his constant eating, his people cut him down until there was nothing left. The moon repeats this story each lunar cycle to remind humans not to be greedy.

In the western Torres Strait, a lunar eclipse is seen as a warning that an enemy army may be coming. The eclipse is called Merlpal Mari Pathanu, which is translated as "a ghost has taken the spirit of the moon." During the eclipse the people hold a ceremony, and they chant the names of the other Torres Strait islands. The one mentioned before the end of the eclipse is where the danger lies.

It is a beautiful
and delightful sight
to behold the body
of the moon.

GALILEO GALILEI

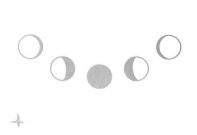

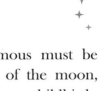

ARTEMIS

Of all the lunar deities the most famous must be Artemis, the Greek goddess not only of the moon, but also of the hunt, the wilderness, nature, childbirth, chastity, wild animals, and nature. She is perhaps the most complex and magnificent of the moon divinities.

As a daughter of Zeus, and twin sister of Apollo, she is most often to be found at the hunt, surrounded by her chaste nymphs. So sacred was she that when a young archer, Actaeon, accidentally saw her bathing naked, she turned him into a stag, and he was torn apart by his own hunting dogs.

No goddess was more venerated than Artemis; temples devoted to her were found across the ancient world. The Temple of Artemis in Ephesus, in modern Turkey, was one of the Seven Wonders of the World. It was over 350 by 180 feet (about 110 by 55 meters) and held some of the greatest art of antiquity.

Legend has it that of the two twins, Artemis and Apollo, it was Artemis who was born first during the night, and she was able to help her mother give birth to Apollo during the next day. This is why she became associated with both the moon and childbirth.

According to the Roman writer Plutarch, Artemis led the Athenians to victory over the Persians at the Battle of Salamis by providing a full moon out of sequence to light the battlefield and terrify the Persian army.

Artemis remains strongly associated with female power, and it is believed by many that Hecate, the queen of witches, is none other than Artemis. When NASA decided in 2017 to reestablish a human presence on the moon for the first time since 1972, there was only one thing they could name it—the Artemis Program.

The moon, like a flower
in heaven's high bower,
with silent delight,
sits and smiles on the night.

William Blake

MAMA KILLA'S TEARS

Of all the phenomena of the moon that the ancients have had to account for, perhaps the lunar eclipse has been the most mysterious. Not only does the moon disappear, it turns the color of blood before doing so.

The Incas of South America, whose empire flourished from the thirteenth to fifteenth century, believed that the moon was the goddess Mama Killa, who cried silver tears. She had married a fox, and the dark spots on the moon was fox's pelt held in her arms.

They thought that lunar eclipses occurred when Mama Killa was attacked by a serpent or a jaguar, and that the world would be plunged into darkness if Mama Killa was to die. So they made as much noise as they could, to frighten off the attacker. When the Spanish conquered the Incas, they were able to use this belief to their advantage—they were able to predict eclipses, winning the respect of the Incas.

THE MOON AND THE WEATHER

For many, the moon gives us secret clues about the future—especially about the weather! The Scots say "clear moon, frost soon," while people of Bedfordshire have been known to warn that "two full moons in a month bring on a flood."

Shetland islanders swear that if you see a halo around the moon, it can mean only one thing, "the moon with a circle brings water in her beak" and so it is going to rain soon. As it rains on the Shetland Islands 243 days a year, they are more often right than wrong.

Sailors are a little more cheerful, stating that a full moon "eats the clouds," bringing fine weather, but ask any farmer and he'll warn you that a full moon at Christmas means the harvest will be poor. This is something to look out for in 2034 when it next happens!

SHEER LUNACY

As is well known, we get our word "lunacy" from the idea that a full moon can drive people mad. In fact, in eighteenth-century England, criminals charged with murder could appeal for lighter sentences if the crime had occurred on the night of a full moon. Meanwhile at the London asylum called Bethlehem, patients were put in shackles to stop them attacking each other and themselves when the moon was full.

Some research has shown that there is a slight lift in crime rates during a full moon, but this has been put down to basic statistics rather than "lunacy"—more people are active during a well-lit night, including criminals, so it only stands to reason there would be more crime.

This is also, they argue, why more pets end up in veterinary surgeries during a full moon—more activity means more possible injuries.

WEREWOLVES

But if scientists have managed to explain the greater crime rates and animal injuries during a full moon, there is one thing they have never explained—werewolves.

Werewolves—men who turn into wolves—have haunted the European imagination since the time of the Greeks, but it was in the Middle Ages that they became associated with the full moon. It is no coincidence that this was at a similar time as the witch trials that swept across Europe.

The reason men turn into werewolves is disputed—heredity, satanic allegiance, being bitten by a wolf, divine punishment, or being cursed by a saint have all been proposed. What is known is that the transformation happens when the moon is full. The transformation is usually involuntary and painful, and if the man returns to human form, he may not remember his time as a wolf. This return is usually at the end of the full moon night.

In fact, the first time the now-famous visual transformation of man into wolf occurs is in the 1943 film, *Frankenstein Meets the Wolf Man*. Produced to cash in on the success of the movies *The Ghost of Frankenstein* and *The Wolf Man*, it received what have been called "lukewarm" reviews. However, it did fix in people's minds the image of a transformation featuring a man howling beneath a full moon as he bursts through his clothes.

Why this happens at a full moon is unclear, although a 2023 article by Phil Plait in *Scientific American* did try to point out that if humans did end up colonizing the moon, there would be a danger that any members of the party who were from werewolf stock might be at risk of permanent transformation and kill everyone else. Imagine the potential transformations if Jupiter or Saturn were colonized, with 95 and 146 moons, respectively!

KAUT AND IAE

The Mamaiurans are an Amazonian tribe who make their home in dense woodlands. But back in the distant past, they believed it was not forests that blocked out the sun, but flocks of birds so dense that no light could reach the Earth. This made the people terrified that they would be attacked by wild animals they could not see.

Two brothers, Kaut and Iae, became fed up and decided to visit Urubutsin, King of the Birds, and beg him to share the daylight with the people of the tribe. The brothers hid inside a dead animal, and when Urubutsin came near, they leapt out and grabbed his leg, refusing to let him go.

In return for his freedom, he agreed that from that day on, day and night would alternate, and that even at night the brightness of the moon would reach them. Kaut now represents the sun, and Iae represents the moon.

MAASAI LEGEND

To the Maasai people of East Africa, the sun and moon are an old married couple who have traveled together forever. The sun is much stronger than the moon, so for three days each month he has to carry the tired moon. The moon disappears but can be seen again on the fourth day by donkeys, and on the fifth by humans.

As we all know, too much travel can be tiring, and one day the moon became tetchy. She and the sun fought a great battle. The sun eventually won, but in doing so he scarred the face of his beautiful wife. The shadows on the moon are her wounds.

The sun was ashamed of himself and wanted to hide from all eyes. He decided to shine so brightly that no one could ever look directly at him. But as we know, this shows the moon's scars even more, no matter how many times she tries to turn away.

RONA, THE TREE, AND THE WATER BUCKET

In Māori culture, there is no rabbit or Man in the Moon. They see a woman named Rona, who one night argued with her husband about who should go and get a bucket of water. Finally, she stormed off into the night, cursing her husband. She was guided by the moonlight, but when the moon went behind a cloud, she stubbed her foot on the roots of a tree. She then turned her curses onto the moon itself.

The moon heard her and punished her by drawing her up into the sky. In fear, Rona grabbed hold of a tree, which was torn from the Earth. When we look at the moon we can see Rona, her water bucket, and the tree trapped on the moon forever.

Some say she and the moon god Marama actually fell in love and she stays there voluntarily. What we do know is that it rains when Rona spills water from her bucket.

THE RED THREAD OF FATE

One day, a young Chinese boy saw an old man in the moonlight, who he did not recognize as Yue Lao, the matchmaker god, who lives under the moon. The man told the boy that he was attached to his one true love by a red thread. He pointed to a small girl and told the boy she was his future wife. The boy threw a rock at her and ran away.

Many years later, the boy grew up and met a beautiful woman and married her. When they reached the wedding chamber, he removed her veil and saw up close a scar on her forehead and realized that she was the girl at whom he had thrown the rock.

It's the job of Yue Lao to seek out future lovers and tie them by the thread. We cannot escape this destiny, and Yue Lao watches over us at all times, waiting to bind us to the one we will love.

THE MOON AND FATE

As Yue Lao and his red thread teaches us, we can never escape our fate once the gods have decided it. But throughout history, many people have believed that we can appeal to the moon to either change it for us or tell us what it is.

For instance, it is said that putting a mirror under your pillow will help you dream of your future love. If you do not, then you are fated to be lonely at least until the next full moon when you can try again.

It is also said that wearing red underwear during a full moon will bring prosperity, but make sure you don't cut your fingernails that night, as that will bring the opposite.

But the full moon can also bring healing. Write what ails you on paper and burn it in fire. Place the ashes in running water and the illness will be washed away with the embers.

THE MIRROR OF AMATERASU

A Japanese legend tells the story of Amaterasu the sun goddess. One day she became angry with her brother Susanoo, the god of storms, and left the sky, plunging the world into darkness.

The people pleaded with the gods to help them, and the gods found the cave in which Amaterasu was hiding, named the Heavenly Rock-Cave. The gods placed a mirror at the entrance of the cave so the light would return to the Earth.

But Amaterasu was vain, and when she saw herself in the mirror, she longed to possess her own reflection. The gods agreed to leave her a mirror for eternity if she would return to light the Earth. She agreed, and the moon is that mirror, which the sun turns in front of, admiring herself.

When the moon disappears, it is the gods reminding Amaterasu not to misbehave again, its blood-red hue showing her that, in anger, we lose the things we love.

ORLANDO FURIOSO

Orlando furioso (*The Frenzy of Orlando*) is an epic written by sixteenth-century poet Ludovico Ariosto and tells stories of King Charlemagne's knights and their many adventures.

One of them, Astolfo, Orlando's cousin, lost his mind, and is told by Saint John the Apostle that it can only be found on the moon. He traveled there by the prophet Elijah's flaming chariot and found that the moon is a dumping ground for all the things that have gone missing from Earth.

He found lots of physical objects that had been lost, but many abstract things too, such as fame, good manners, broken promises, and the sighs and tears of lovers. And of course, his sanity, which he finds locked inside a bottle.

There is one thing he could not find anywhere on the moon, and that is foolishness—because all human foolishness remains here on Earth.

THE BAMBOO CUTTER

We think of people who come from the moon as a recent invention of science fiction. But as long ago as 800 CE, one Chinese tale spoke of just this.

One day a childless old man out cutting bamboo discovered a tiny three-inch girl among the stalks. He took her home, and he and his wife took care of her, and she quickly grew to normal size. They named her Nayotake no Kaguya-hime (Shining Princess of the Young Bamboo).

But as happy as she was with the old couple, every night she went out into the darkness and stared up at the moon. Tears filled her eyes, night after night.

Eventually they all realized the moon was her home. The old man assembled a large troop of helpers, and by climbing the tallest mountain they were able to return Kaguya-hime home. Now she gazes at Earth and tears fill her eyes, but she is where she belongs.

THE LOVE OF THE SUN FOR THE MOON

Long ago, the sun was first worshipped by humans as a bringer of light and of fertility. It was well known that all the plants on Earth grew in the light of the sun. We eat these plants to keep us alive, so everyone, every day, came out to worship him. But when the moon came out all the people would go inside and close their eyes until it was time for the sun again.

The sun loved the moon and wanted her worshipped like he was. He knew the moon was timid, so he decided all he could do was show her in his own light, and when she was glowing, he would disappear so the stage would be her own.

He has done this night after night for many years. People now worship the moon as much as they worship the sun. And sometimes they share the sky, which are precious moments for them both.

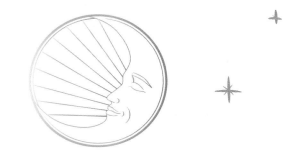

Don't worry if
you're making waves
just by being yourself.
The moon does it
all the time.

SCOTT STABILE

CHAPTER THREE

MOON SPELLS

Now that we've come to know the moon, through stories, myths, and legends, how do we invite it into our lives and let it help us in our dark moments and our light?

Throughout history, sages of the moon have learned spells and magic that allow us to harness its beauty and power.

There are spells for love, spells for happiness, and spells for good fortune. There are also spells that help us find ourselves, and which we can give as gifts to those we love. There are spells for the new moon, the full moon, and the phases in between.

This is a new journey for you, and an old one for the moon.

HOW TO START

Before you try to tap into the beauty and power of the moon, it is important to make sure you prepare yourself to enter a state of acceptance. For many of us, our day-to-day lives are full of demands, worries, and noise. We can try to shut these things off too quickly and become frustrated when they still press upon us.

The solution is to be gentle with yourself. Moon spells are never quick fixes, although sometimes miracles do occur. Accept that letting the moon in is a process, not an event. Expecting instant results can lead to resistance, and the moon can sense this and take itself away from you. Don't worry, it is still always there, but you will have to invite it back with gratitude and humility.

Gradually let go of the noise of the day, and if that takes you all night or all week, then so be it. The moon isn't going anywhere. It has waited this long.

WHEN TO START

For many people the ideal time to start casting spells with the moon is either when it is full or when it is new. These are the times when spells can be most powerful, and the effects most dramatic.

But always remember the old saying, "The best time to plant a tree was 20 years ago, the second-best time is now." If you want to start your cosmic journey, start it now, whichever phase of the moon is in the night sky. If you regret not starting at the last new moon, and think you'll wait until the next, who knows what might get in the way. You don't want to spend another 29.5 days waiting.

Because, as we have learned, the moon is always the same moon, each phase just brings out one or another aspect of it. So tonight's moon is when to start!

WHERE TO START

As with "How to Start," the best can often be the enemy of the good when thinking of where to start your moon rituals. Wherever you are you can access the power of the moon.

But as we all know, the more you can commit to something, the greater the results—and this is you committing to you! Take some time to find a space that is uncluttered by the everyday, a place where you can be silent and concentrate.

This is your time, shut the door, turn off your phone and make a space for yourself so you can relax. So much of your time is spent looking after others, now your only task is to look after yourself.

And if you feel any guilt at locking the world outside your door, remember that the more centered you are, the more you can provide the world with the care and support you wish to give.

KEEPING A CALENDAR

It seems a simple thing, but keeping a calendar that shows the phases of the moon can help you approach your spells more directly. Some calendars go into great detail about the phases, and contain information about eclipses, where the moon is in relation to the sun (the perigee or apogee—near or far away) and symbols to show which star sign is dominant, which is ascendant, and which is in the midheavens.

But even the simplest calendar with just the phases marked will do.

Some people choose to keep their calendar in the place they do their spells, while some prefer to place it in a domestic space as a reminder that there is much going on outside the house. Stick it somewhere you can see often, to remember whatever the day holds, the moon is on course, and you will be spending time with it soon.

MAKING AN ALTAR

Many people who perform moon spells set up an altar. This is a collection of objects that is meaningful to them. An altar can be as simple as a single burning candle or a bowl of water. Or it can be populated with pictures of friends and family, or aromatic spices, or a favorite doll, or flowers or incense. Even the most mundane objects can find a place if they are meaningful and bring you solace or peace.

Altars are dynamic things, they can change depending on the spell, or change depending on yourself. If your altar doesn't feel right, the answer is simple—alter it!

Remember your altar is part of your process, so even the building of it should be an act of reverence. Take your time, move things, add things, and take them away. When it is as you wish it, give thanks for its power. It is your still point on your cosmic journey.

KEEPING A JOURNAL

As with many practices of self-improvement and self-care, keeping a journal can be an important part of your celestial journey. By keeping a record of our process, we help to manifest it, and to make ourselves aware of some of the parts of the journey that may not appear to us without the act of externalizing, of writing down.

The great thing about journaling is that there is no right or wrong way to do it—the journal is for you and nobody else. It can be brief thoughts, lists, or detailed explorations of steps on your journey. By keeping this record, you will be more readily able to identify patterns and see progress. Sometimes it is easy to forget how far you have traveled—a journal will help you remember.

There is only one thing a journal requires from you and that is honesty. By allowing yourself to be open, you'll be amazed at the things that come rushing in to help!

BUILDING
YOUR JOURNEY

Sometimes a moon spell is simply something to do when the mood takes you, or you feel the need. There is nothing wrong with that, the moon won't mind! But by getting into good habits, you can make your interaction with the moon build and grow.

Here are a few things you might wish to do, whichever spell you are hoping to cast.

1. Before any ritual, think through what you want it to achieve. This will help you bring focus and clarity.

2. If you've made an altar (see page 72), set it in such a way that it represents the intentions of your ritual that day.

3. Clear your mind. As we have seen, the world will always try to rush in with its clutter. Sometimes getting clear is just a matter of letting go, but some people like to use music, visualization, or essential oils as part of this process. Do whatever works for you!

4. Speak, sing, or write your purpose or intention clearly. This is not just so they are heard by the moon, but so that they are heard by you as well. It can be difficult sometimes to know what we want, and if we do know, it can be difficult to allow ourselves to say it out loud. This is your chance.

5. Focus on the ritual in the way that works best for you. For some this is just a part of the silence, for others, drumming, singing, or chanting helps anchor the ritual in the self. If you find yourself wanting to do these things, don't hold back!

6. Ground your energies. Touch the Earth literally and figuratively.

7. Give thanks. The moon does not ask for thanks but this is powerful in the giving rather than the receiving.

8. Decompress. Go for a walk, breathe deeply, write in your journal (see page 73), or yell out in joy. Whatever works for you!

GREETING THE NEW MOON

As we have seen, the new moon is about beginnings, setting goals, and making them manifest. By making the moon your partner in this quest, you can lean on its power and use it to help you make your dreams a reality.

A simple way to greet the new moon is to spend some time outside in its presence. Take a notebook, a candle, a small glass of water and a pen. Set down your intentions for the next 29 days. Include the things you wish to bring into your life, and the things you want to exclude. When you read these back you should feel a tingle of truth—you will feel it through your body.

Light the candle, drink the water, and take a moment to reflect. Just as the water suffuses your body, and the candle smoke curls into the air, so your intentions reach inside you, and join with the celestial.

The next night, follow the same process, but don't take the pen. It is time for you to live with your intentions, take them from inside yourself, project them out into the universe, and start to make them manifest. As you breathe, feel yourself manifesting—breathe in and draw your intentions down, breathe out and send them into the universe. Breathe slowly and steadily.

For some people, reciting their intentions out loud helps make them real. Over the course of the next month take the time to recite them, even if it's just in your mind.

If one of your intentions no longer feels right, make a mental note to cross it out. This is a process of refining. You and your intentions are becoming one.

Again, light the candle and drink the water and reflect on the relationship of all things. One is fire, one is water, and yet both are you.

NEW MOON—
THE WITCH'S CAULDRON

Is there anything more healing than a nice hot bath? It can be a time to relax with a scented candle, some quiet music and bath salts and forget about all the troubles of the day.

But for us, a bath at the new moon can be so much more than this—the bath is our very own witch's cauldron in which we can do magic. If you can see the new moon through the window, so much the better.

As you lower yourself into the bath, feel yourself enveloped by the cleansing water and salt. Then allow yourself to think through the things you want to be rid of. This can be painful—if it gets too much take a moment to reengage with the water.

Think about how the hurt comes off you and how it will be washed away when you pull the plug—it will go down the drain and you will be free.

NEW MOON CRYSTAL SPELL

It is well known that crystals can perform miracles in our earthly journey, but it is less well known that the moon can be used to reinvigorate them.

The new moon is kindred with crystals associated with inspiration, creativity, and success—clear or rose quartz, citrine, lapis lazuli, and obsidian. Each of these crystals has the power to manifest our intentions and to cleanse our souls.

1. At the new moon place one or more of these crystals in the soft moonlight.

2. Speak your intentions to them three, six or nine times.

3. Leave them overnight.

4. When you collect them, thank the moon for infusing them with its power.

5. You can then either carry the crystals with you or place them on your altar.

Repeat this ritual at each new moon and feel the power of the crystals grow as your intentions become real.

NEW MOON PROSPERITY SPELL

The new moon is a great time to reassess your finances, and this simple spell can help increase prosperity.

1. Set up your altar to attract prosperity. This means adding green candles that represent fire, surrounded by your crystals, which represent the Earth. In addition to your new moon crystals (see page 79) you might also include amethyst and jade.

2. Light the candles and burn some prosperity herbs—cinnamon, mint, clover, and ginger. These represent the air.

3. Add the fourth element by drinking moon water (see page 91).

4. Write yourself a prosperity check, showing you are open to the abundance of the universe. Put the amount you truly want, not a fantasy number.

5. Date your check, sign it and place it somewhere where you can read it each day.

6. If your amount was realistic, the universe will provide; if not, try again next new moon!

The Moon was but a Chin of Gold

A Night or two ago—

And now she turns Her perfect Face

Upon the World below.

Emily Dickinson

WAXING MOON SPELLS

As we know, a waxing moon, including the first quarter moon, is characterized by increasing. It is the next step in the journey to manifesting your desires, such as prosperity, luck, career, love, or fertility.

The waxing moon is always giving off strong manifesting energy—it wants to give! One fun spell is to go outside to the waxing moon and simply ask for "something unexpected." If the new moon is when we focus on the things we know we need, the waxing moon can surprise us with gifts we didn't know we needed or wanted. These might be frivolous, like a smile from a stranger or an idea for a project, or more serious, like new love or an unexpected child. In this way, the moon reminds us to be open and to give over our desires to it for a moment and see what it brings.

WAXING MOON BAY LEAF SPELL

This is a great way to make your intentions manifest, and all you need is a bay leaf, a pen, a match, and the light of the waxing moon.

1. On the bay leaf, write down what you want to make manifest.

2. Place the bay leaf on the palm of your hand and hold it out to the moon.

3. Feel the moon's energy moving through the bay leaf and into your body.

4. Bring the bay leaf to your chest and visualize what you want to manifest, or say it out loud.

5. When you can clearly visualize the thing you want, or the person you want to be, bring the bay leaf inside and burn it on your altar.

6. Visualize the smoke rising to the moon, carrying your desires.

7. You can let the bay leaf burn out naturally. The spell is complete when you discard the ashes.

WAXING MOON
SPELL FOR APHRODITE

If we want to increase anything, surely the most important thing is love.

The waxing moon is the ideal time to call on Aphrodite, the goddess of love, and this spell will bring her to you, and maybe someone you desire.

1. Gather as many *edible* flowers as you can—older spells will tell you they have to be pink, but these days any color can manifest love. Roses are good because of their deep connection with love, but choose flowers that are edible and mean something personal to you.

2. In hot water, mix together foods of love—cinnamon, honey, and vanilla—to make an herbal brew. Add your chosen flower petals.

3. Cast a circle of flower petals, candles, and crystals, and then invite Aphrodite in.

4. Drink your brew while you contemplate love and romance. Ask for Aphrodite's help.

5. Finish your brew and then close the circle by taking it apart in reverse order. Thank Aphrodite and let her leave.

FULL MOON SPELLS

The full moon exerts the most powerful magic. Even those who don't believe in the moon as magical can feel the full moon's effects. For those who do, its power can be harnessed in many ways. Moon water gains more strength from the full moon, while crystals can soak up its celestial power more easily.

While the new moon is about anticipation and planning, the full moon is about the moment. This is a simple ritual that can be observed without any preparation and has been used by cultures across all time. Just go outside, put on your favorite music and dance beneath the full moon. Embrace the moment without shame, without carrying the past or looking to the future. Shake off the old you and live in the present. If you do this once every 29 days, the other 28 will never seem a burden.

FULL MOON SCRYING

"Scrying" means looking into the future, usually by looking into a mirror or as in this case, the reflection in water.

1. Perform any personal rituals to clear a space to welcome the moon. Feel its energy and its silver light.

2. Have ready a pitcher of water, a dark-colored bowl, and your journal.

3. Close your eyes until you are ready, then open them and feel clarity and awareness.

4. Slowly pour the water from the pitcher into the bowl, watching the moonlight making it sparkle.

5. Stare into the water, looking for patterns, symbols, or pictures. You may see images moving, you may see words forming.

6. Write down everything you see in your journal, and every thought you have. The meaning may not reveal itself immediately.

7. When you have finished, perform any actions you need to get closure.

Revisit the journal often—you will be amazed at the things that it will reveal.

FULL MOON SPELL TO REVEAL WHAT IS HIDDEN

This is a time-honored spell, and all you need is a bowl of cherries. Cherries are said to have mystical powers and share a characteristic with the moon. They both hide something—the moon hides its dark side, and the cherry hides its pit.

This spell is therefore about revealing what is hidden.

1. With a bowl of cherries, sit down by the window so you can see the full moon.

2. Ask the moon to show you what is hidden.

3. Eat the cherries and drop each cherry pit back into the bowl.

4. After you finish all the cherries, stir the pits with your left hand, then discard the pits.

5. The juice from the pits will have left a pattern in the bowl, and in it you may see the solution to a mystery. Look for shapes, images, or symbols and journal about any thoughts or messages you receive.

SLEEPING UNDER A FULL MOON

This is not a spell, although the effects can be magical. As is well known, a full moon is suffused with healing energy, as is sleep. So when the two are combined, the power is doubled—maybe even tripled!

It is the simplest thing you can do—just go out somewhere safe in the open on the night of a full moon and sleep for a short while—even an hour will work wonders and help restore you.

Some people say they have trouble sleeping during a full moon, but that is because they are trying to push the moon away. In a fight with a full moon, there can only be one winner. So, in this ritual, don't lie there trying to sleep—instead let the moon enter into you and guide your descent into dreams.

On waking, write down what the night has taught you. But be warned, sleeping under the full moon is wonderfully addictive! You will find yourself at one with the universe, and with your deeper self.

FULL MOON POPPET LOVE SPELL

Poppets are little dolls that can be used to represent a person. In this full moon love spell, you will need two: one to represent yourself, one to represent the person of your desires. Ideally you should place something that belongs to your love inside the poppet, like an item of jewelry or a photograph.

1. Perform any preparations you feel you need for moon spells. Put the rest of the world away.

2. Say to the first poppet, "I made you, and your name is (insert the name of the beloved)."

3. Repeat for the other but use your own name.

4. Take a pink ribbon and tie the two poppets together.

5. Hold both poppets in your hands and visualize your happy life together.

6. Hold them up to the full moon and thank the moon for helping with this union.

7. If the moon recognizes the union as genuine and true, then you will find a way to manifest it. If you can't, then the moon knew there was something wrong.

FULL MOON FERTILITY SPELL

As we know, the full moon is associated with fertility, and children are conceived more easily under its watch. This spell uses two other fertility symbols—an egg and a fig.

1. Place a clear glass bowl in the middle of a table, with an egg to the left of it and a fig to the right.

2. Light a white candle and a stick of frankincense. Place both on the table above the bowl.

3. Carefully crack the egg into the bowl, and add the seeds of the fig, scooped out with a spoon.

4. Put the rest of the fig into the eggshell to represent the child in the womb.

5. Stir the mixture in the bowl with your finger three times. Say, "As two become one, may our union be blessed with a child."

6. Bury the spell ingredients as the full moon bathes the Earth in its light.

MAKING MOON WATER

As the name suggests, moon water is water that has been infused with the power of the moon. It is best to do this at the full moon, to take in the greatest power of the moon, but even the weakest moon water contains more power than can be imagined.

The process is simple.

1. Before you sleep, place a container of water on your windowsill. This works best if the container is glass, so the moon can enter the water from all angles. Some people keep a special glass for this, but the moon finds what is left out for it.

2. Sleep—if you can! As we have seen the full moon loves our company and can try to keep us awake.

3. In the morning, you can either drink the water or use it for spells. It can even give your plants a boost!

4. Dry the glass gently but thoroughly and place it upside down in your cupboard.

BLOOD MOON RITUAL— THE EVIL EYE

During a blood moon, it is best to stay inside, and keep away from those who might cause psychic harm. It can also be the time to find out if anyone has been sending you bad vibes, also known as the evil eye, as in this spell.

1. Pour moon water (see page 91) into a bowl and light two matches.

2. While the matches are alight, think of the person you believe may have been giving you the evil eye and then drop the matches into the water.

3. If the matches touch each other or land in the shape of an X, then that person has been sending you the evil eye.

4. If they stay apart, they haven't.

Remember, this only works when there is a blood moon, so you need to act quickly. But it can be a great way to identify and rid yourself of those who mean you harm.

WANING MOON SPELLS-
CORD CUTTING

The waning moon, including the final quarter moon, is a perfect time to explore acceptance, and for transitioning and completing your goals. It can also be a time to detox your house, your body and to get rid of those people or things that are holding you back.

One thing you may need to get rid of is an ex-partner, and this spell is best done as the moon wanes.

1. Gather a black candle, black yarn, and a cup or bowl.

2. Light the candle.

3. Bind your wrists loosely with the cord and think about the way holding onto your ex holds you back from happiness.

4. Allow the cord to soak up the negative energy.

5. Now cut the cord and say "I release these ties that bind."

6. Burn the cord in a vessel. You have sent away the negativity and are free.

WANING MOON PET PROTECTION SPELL

Let's not forget those companions who can be as precious to us as any human—our pets. Just as the waning moon is good for getting rid of the things that affect us negatively, it is also a time to draw close to the things we love. This spell places a ring of protection around your familiars.

1. Light a brown candle, which symbolizes animals and nurturing, near a glass of moon water.

2. Place a picture of your beloved pet next to it.

3. Ask the moon to protect your pet and keep it from harm.

4. Sprinkle a few drops of water on the picture.

5. Let the candle burn for a few moments, then blow it out.

6. Cut the burned tip of the candle and bury it with the picture in the garden or a flowerpot.

You can now either drink the water or use it to water the place you planted the picture.

It's the moon
that moves me.
The sunlight makes
everything so obvious.

BAVO DHOOGE

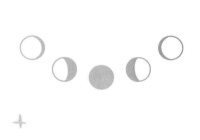

CHAPTER FOUR

MOON MEDITATIONS

There are many ways to connect with the moon, but perhaps the deepest one is through meditation. By turning inward, we draw the moon with us, and by emptying our minds we allow it to inhabit the open space within. As with every relationship with the moon, it is subject to change as the moon moves through its phases, but still behind the changing aspects of the moon remains the stable object on which to turn our thoughts. And the more we open ourselves to the moon, the more we open ourselves to our own possibilities.

WHAT IS MOON MEDITATION?

Moon meditation is a practice that involves meditating during the specific phases of the moon. This way we can tap into its energy more directly and allow it to shape our feelings and emotions, our plans and expectations. It is a way to make our relationship with the moon intimate, and to call on all its powers of wisdom and healing.

It can also help you tap into your inner wisdom and intuition, which can help you make better choices and navigate your way through life with more confidence. We also know how the power of the moon can help us manifest our desires and intentions, and moon meditation only deepens that experience.

And finally, moon meditation can help us sleep—as the moon's cycles come into sync with our sleep cycles, we can use them to climb the ladder down into dreams, and up again into a refreshing day.

LEARNING TO MEDITATE

Meditation is an ancient practice of mindfulness, where the mind is focused on a particular object, activity or thought to achieve a state of peace and calm. It has been practiced for many hundreds of years, but the basic tenets have remained the same.

First, find a quiet place to meditate, free from distractions. Close your eyes, relax your body, and empty your mind. Focusing on your breathing can help with this. Pay attention to the thoughts and feelings that occur, without trying to change them. If your mind starts to wander, bring it back to your breath. You can also use an object or a mantra to help you stay focused.

Now gradually expand your awareness to include the sensations in your body, and the sounds around you. Again, embrace everything that arises without judging. You are now in a meditative state.

GUIDED MEDITATION

Another form of meditation is guided meditation and this can be especially beneficial to beginners.

As the name suggests, in guided meditation a teacher is there to take us through the ritual. They can help us find the space within ourselves where inner peace resides, and gently bring us back to the right path when our mind starts to wander. A guide will help you stay focused and relaxed during your meditation.

Guided meditation can also be done in groups, and this can be particularly fruitful when it comes to moon meditation. After all, the moon is there for us all to share, and the power of the moon can be made all the greater when it moves through many people. This is why tribes dance and drum at the full moon.

MOON MEDITATION– HOW TO BEGIN

As with spells, there is no time like the present to welcome the moon into your life. But be aware that meditation is not something that can be rushed. There is no point trying to meditate if you are thinking about how quickly you need to be finished.

However, most practitioners recommend that you start with just ten minutes a day, and gradually build your practice up. One reason for this is to allow someone who hasn't made meditation a regular part of their schedule time to get started.

The other is that meditation can only be mastered slowly, and there will be days when the desired state cannot be reached. This can be discouraging, especially if a lot of time has been set aside. Better that these sessions are brief and try again tomorrow. Practice makes perfect!

MOON MEDITATION—
THE FIRST TIME

It may be that you practice some meditation before moving your focus to the moon, but it is not strictly necessary to do so. Some people even find that they adapt more quickly to meditation if they have this focus. And of all the objects we might meditate on, what could be more familiar than the moon?

As with any meditation, it is important to find a comfortable place to meditate, somewhere where there is peace and quiet. Ideally, it would be a place that allows the moon to be seen, but as we know, the moon doesn't stay still so finding a spot where it can always be seen can be impossible. But try to make sure you precede the meditation by looking at the moon, even if only for a few moments. Drink in what it looks like.

Once you have found your place and seen the moon, follow the normal steps for meditation, letting go of harmful thoughts, opening up your mind, and allowing what comes to the surface to come to the surface, without judgment.

Now it is time to bring the moon into it, but for your first few sessions, don't feel pressured to make anything happen—later we will meditate in ways that will help us manifest and heal. For now, we are getting to know the moon and feel the way it resonates inside us. Try to bring the moon you have just seen to mind, or if you are able to see it, make that the moon you focus on. We want to tap into each phase of the moon.

After your ten minutes, allow yourself to slowly surface. Of course, if the place you are in is making you happy and strong, linger for a while. This is where you want to be.

MEDITATING WITH THE PHASES OF THE MOON

Good basic meditation practices will become the bedrock of your moon meditation practice. As you gradually grow in confidence with the process, you will find it easier to reach a meditative state and grow more comfortable staying in it for longer. Keep tuning yourself to the phases of the moon by observing it directly or calling it to mind as part of your focus.

By now you will be familiar with the phases of the moon, what they mean and what they represent. Moon meditation attempts to harness the significance of each phase and draw it down into our being. When we become one with a particular phase of the moon, we come to be a part of what the moon is and share in its dynamic form. From the new moon to the full moon and back again, our meditations draw from the strength of our lunar friend.

NEW MOON MEDITATION— WIPING AWAY THE DARKNESS

The new moon marks a new beginning, and some have said that the lunar cycle is like the universe taking a deep breath. With every new moon, nature exhales, pausing before the next inhalation. As we know, it is a time to recognize new intentions, and to draw on the power of the moon to make them manifest.

The new moon is the best time to start meditating, but it can also be the most confronting. In the absence of moonlight, the sky is much darker, and for some people this darkness mirrors their own darkness inside, their memories and emotions.

But remember, the new moon will grow to wipe away that darkness, just as you will wipe away the darkness through your practices of meditation. If it becomes too much, seek guidance, but have faith in the moon to share its journey to the light.

MANIFESTING INTENTIONS

During meditation, as we have seen, it is important to let whatever decides to come to mind arrive without judgment. Moon meditation is no different, except we learn to harness these thoughts as the meditation progresses to help us on the journey to selfhood. Each meditation should be directed toward a goal of self-realization.

Set the intention of your meditation before you begin, in the same way that you set your intentions in your journal. Remember the new moon is about fresh beginnings, clean breaks, and the planning of future projects. Decide on one intention you wish to call on the moon to help with and keep this in mind as you move into meditation.

Don't worry if there is more than one thing you want— if you cannot bring them all to your meditation, there is another new moon just around the corner!

NEW MOON MEDITATIONS-
AFFIRMATIONS

As we start to meditate on the new moon, our mind will open to all sorts of feelings, thoughts, and emotions. Let it do so. The answers to our questions are not always obvious—that's why they are questions! Allow your mind to drift among these sensations and record what is needed for its own work.

Gradually begin to move your mind toward the intention of this meditation. Sometimes this is a slow process, and the mind can go off on other journeys. Don't pull the reins too tight, your mind and the moon know what they are doing.

But sometimes it can happen quickly, as you become aware that the seemingly random sensations are in fact guiding your goal. Wrap these thoughts in affirmations about new beginnings, about love, success, and positivity. The more you do this, the more you become open to the universe, and the more your intentions become manifest.

NEW MOON MANIFESTATION— LETTING GO

As you perform your affirmations, leave room for letting go of the things you no longer need, the memories that cause pain, and the things that stop you achieving your goals. You may be surprised at how easily this can happen—it is like your mind has a mind of its own! Often the simple act of affirming something valuable to you will wash away something destructive. You might even see it fall away without feeling any hurt—deep down you knew it had to go.

Keep concentrating on those things you wish to manifest. As we know from journaling and speaking our intentions out loud, the more we manifest our intentions, the more real they become, and the more likely we are to achieve them. The meditative state is there to be open to a world of possibilities. Let them in!

NEW MOON MEDITATION— SURFACING

As with all meditation practices, make sure you surface gradually and at your own pace. Sometimes you may wish to linger, sometimes you feel a sense of achievement so powerful that you want to get to the end and celebrate. Either is fine—you will know what to do.

As you come out of meditation, keep concentrating on your breathing, as it forms a ladder back to full consciousness. When you emerge, keep in a relaxed pose, and don't try to move away too quickly—reality can be discombobulating after deep meditation!

Now is the time to reflect on the whole experience, and to explore with your conscious mind in what ways your intentions were achieved. Every meditation will effect some change, and it is important to take a moment to acknowledge that. Think about the session or journal it. Like dreams, meditative states can slip away too quickly. Capture it while you can.

BREATHE IN
BREATHE OUT

We have already heard how the lunar month has been compared to the universe breathing in and out in a constant cycle. In moon meditation, our breathing practices not only bring us to a meditative state, they mimic and share in the very motion of the universe.

Sometimes called "breath work," we are called upon to focus all of our attention on something we rarely think about: our breathing. When we meditate, the rhythm of our breath becomes important, and we are encouraged to breathe slowly and deeply—so deeply that it is our diaphragm that expands and contracts more than our chest.

The great thing about breath work is you can't really do it wrong—after all we've been doing it our entire lives—and can say with some certainty we will until the end! It is the act of focusing on our breathing that is all important, not how we are breathing.

However, as we deepen our meditation practices, so we can embrace more sophisticated breathing techniques. Practice breathing deep down to your diaphragm, so your belly expands like a balloon—or a gibbous moon—as you inhale, and as you breathe out feel your belly button move back toward your spine— like a crescent.

Another technique is to hold each breath for a few moments after inhaling and exhaling—Navy SEALs are trained to do this to stay calm in a crisis. Or there is the 4-7-8 technique: inhale through your nose for a count of 4, hold your breath for a count of 7, and then exhale through your mouth for a count of 8. Some studies have shown this to reduce anxiety and breathlessness.

In the end it is up to you how you breathe. The main thing is that you make the breath your focus.

When I admire the wonders of a sunset or the beauty of the moon, my soul expands in the worship of the creator.

Mahatma Gandhi

WAXING MOON MEDITATION

As we have explored, the waxing moon is a time of increase, and by aligning with it through meditation we can increase our own power and overcome resistances. We can also take stock of our goals, those of the lunar month and further into the future. As with any moon meditation it is important to find a quiet place, and to have as much contact with the moon as possible. Get outside under the night sky if you can.

Begin to meditate with a goal in mind, but also bring your desire for abundance—an abundance you deserve. Be open to where your meditation takes you; by now a lot of the negative thoughts and feelings will have left or become manageable, and you will be immersed in a sea of positivity. Bring the waxing moon to mind, as crescent, quarter, or gibbous, and think of its growth toward fullness, recalling you are doing the same.

WAXING MOON MEDITATION— VALUING IMPERFECTION

To some there is another side to the waxing moon, and that is its perfect imperfection. Where the full moon is a perfect sphere, the waxing moon is characterized by its odd shapes. It is on its monthly course to become full, and it does not care how it looks and yet it remains beautiful.

One meditation for the waxing moon is to appreciate that the idea perfection is sometimes a veil which doesn't allow us to see the beauty in imperfection, our own and that of others, and of nature itself. Like the Japanese tea ceremony of *wabi-cha*, which deliberately uses rustic cups, so waxing moon meditation embraces the joy of the flawed.

Because as we know, every imperfect moon hides a perfect one, it is just a matter of perspective, so embrace the joys of imperfection!

FULL MOON MEDITATION

In meditation, we come into contact not only with the sacred energies that flow all around us, but also those that are within—our own sacred energies.

As can be imagined, nothing brings these energies to the fore like the light of the full moon. Its power lights up the night sky, and in lighting us up it is no less powerful.

In each of our meditations we have tried to look upon the moon, but it has not always been possible. But if there is one time to brave the outside world and meditate beneath the open sky, it is the time of the full moon. Even if you only experience it once, you will find all becomes illuminated and all becomes clear. You may find once will turn into twice, because this meditation will keep drawing you back.

FULL MOON MEDITATION—GRATITUDE

In our everyday lives, we can forget to stop and think that the full moon we gaze upon is the same one our neolithic ancestors gazed upon, that Buddha, Jesus, the Prophets, Vyasa, and Mohammed gazed upon, and that Shakespeare, Cleopatra, Ghandi, Einstein and Mozart gazed upon.

Before we meditate on the full moon it is good to show our gratitude that the moon persists, and that we are there to join the famous, the infamous, the ordinary and the extraordinary who have held it in their sight.

It is also a time to give gratitude for our own existence. No matter how many have gazed upon the full moon, we are still one of the very few to have been granted life. We approach the full moon in awe of it and of ourselves, and marvel at how miraculous it is we both exist.

FULL MOON MEDITATION—LOVE

This meditation is not about finding love—there are spells for that, such as the spell on page 84—but for deepening your relationship with the partner who shares your life.

Rather than going out to meditate to the full moon alone, go with your partner. Sit facing each other and begin your meditation. Concentrate on taking your breaths at the same time and keeping eye contact. In this way, you'll draw the power of the moon down into you simultaneously, and it will flow through you in rhythm.

And, because the full moon illuminates those things that are usually hidden, you may find yourself reigniting the passion and excitement in your relationship that may have gone missing.

Of course, if these emotions aren't missing in your relationship, you may end up experiencing an overload of them. But is it possible to have an overload of love?

FULL MOON MEDITATION—FLOWING

As with any moon meditation, it is important to go into any session with an intention you wish to manifest, and full moon meditation is no different. It is more powerful though, so in the interplay between you and the moon it may be best to let it take over if you feel it is heading somewhere new. As ever, never doubt the wisdom of the moon. It has been doing this a lot longer than you have.

As we know, the full moon can also seek out that which is hidden, and sometimes these are needs and desires we didn't know we had. Journaling after a full moon can be an exhilarating experience, as the moon reveals to us new plans and undoes some of the knots that had prevented us from acting. So, as you start to meditate to the full moon, don't be afraid to go with the flow—who knows where you may end up?

FULL MOON MEDITATION-HEALTH

As anyone who has felt the full moon on their skin can tell you, the full moon is a bringer of radiance and health. Start one of your full moon meditations with the intention of overcoming an illness, or bringing yourself to a new level of health, then imagine the moonlight enveloping and purifying your mind, body, and spirit.

The moon is no miracle worker, of course, but what the moon can do is offer new paths forward. Sometimes these will genuinely cure the symptoms, but other times the full moon will take you deeper, and seek causes you may never have considered, or strategies for managing what ails you that will give new freedom.

To emerge from this meditation can mean emerging from the darkness into the light, and your skin will feel a glow, long after you have retired to your bed and bade the moon goodnight.

FULL MOON MEDITATION—
MANIFESTATION RITUAL

While the moon is full, you can often supercharge some of your manifestation rituals—the moon is filled with energy, it needs something to do!

Form an altar beneath the luminous glow of the full moon, and place on it objects representing your pressing concerns; photos, notes, books, and things that enhance your spiritual power, such as crystals and moon water.

As you meditate, focus on each of those things, and allow the moon to enter into your thoughts. Discuss with the moon what you want to manifest. As you will know through your meditation, this discussion can be wordless or oblique, but you will both understand each other.

Then visualize exactly what you want and send it up to the moon. In doing this, you offer a blueprint to the universe of who you are and what you want. And the universe is the great giver to those who deserve it.

FULL MOON MEDITATION— THE RELEASE

For this meditation you will need a lit candle, a pen and paper, and two bowls, one empty and one full of water.

Go out to the full moon and begin your meditation practice in the way to which you have become accustomed, and this night make the release of negative energy your goal. As you meditate reflect on the things you wish to do away with, the things that hold you back or draw you away from your desires.

Once you have meditated, use the light of the full moon to illuminate the paper as you write down the things you wish to release. When you have finished writing your list, burn the paper with the candle, and let the ashes drop in the empty bowl. Then wash your hands clean in the bowl of water, charging it with positivity.

Once you have finished take a few moments to bask in the miracle of the moon and yourself.

FULL MOON MEDITATION— HARVEST MOON

The harvest moon is perhaps the moon most associated with change. As one year's sowing is gathered in, so the ground is prepared for the next. It is a time to give thanks for the bountiful gifts that nature provides, and to share them with the community.

So it is that when we meditate on the harvest moon, we are invited to take stock of what we have sowed that year and reap the rewards we have been granted. Even in a year of bad harvests, there is always one crop that has survived and prospered, and the harvest moon will direct us to remember it.

But it is also a meditation practice we should allow to look outside of ourselves, to the community we share and the environment we inhabit. Self-realization is not just about the self, because the self is made up of all that is around us. Harvest moon meditation is part of a harvest festival, to which we invite everyone we can.

WANING MOON MEDITATION

For some the waning moon can sometimes be the lesser cousin of the waxing moon, the latter bursting with hope where the former seeks to sum up. But in meditation, the waning moon comes into its own.

For meditation is ultimately contemplation, some of it conscious and some of it subconscious, and the waning moon is the most contemplative moon of all.

In the light of the waning moon, we take stock of both our triumphs and our adversities. It is a time of deep learning, about ourselves and those around us, about nature and fate.

In reaching a meditative state, we give up some of our conscious control and open our minds to all possibilities. We may discover things about ourselves or consider options for our future we never considered before.

In approaching a waning moon meditation, we ask the moon to give us its wisdom. We open ourselves to it, without judgment, as we unite ourselves with the moon.

TAKING STOCK

And so in meditating to the waning moon, we end the lunar cycle as we began, in outer darkness—but by the gift of our practices, we are now suffused with inner light. Those things that had been unclear have become clear, those things that blocked our path have been dismissed, and the abundance that is our birthright has filled us with hope and plenty.

And just as with the cycles of the lunar month, meditation is world without end—the more we meditate the deeper we go, and the more open we become to the rhythms of the universe. But just as the moon pauses each cycle to take stock, so should we.

For the final time we say goodbye and give thanks to the moon, now just a thin sliver in the sky. It is about to leave us for a night or two, and then be born again.

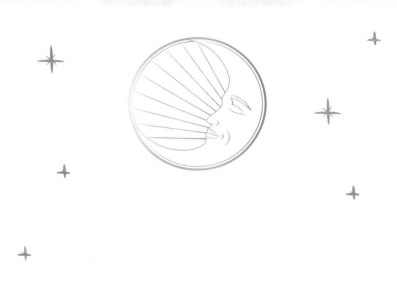

Stay wild,
moon child.

LAST WORD

And so to bed.

The moon has taken us on a journey, across time and space, and deep into our own selves. An object of fascination for scientists, philosophers, and astronomers; an ambition for astronauts; a god or goddess for the religious; a companion for the lover; a mother for nature; and a wonder to anyone who has taken the time to look.

We started by saying how the moon is given to surprising us—appearing where we don't expect it and changing shape each and every night—but even as we find out more, it becomes no less surprising. Born of the Earth, the moon has been our constant and nearest companion for billions of years, shaping our seas and our destinies. And the moon will abide even when the brief candle of our own existence ends. The moon may mourn us, but we shall never mourn the moon.

We have learned that the moon does more than just spin around the sun—it can do magic for us, both in the outside world and in ourselves. By trusting the moon, be it waxing, waning, quarter, new or full, we can align ourselves with the power of the cosmos, lending our shoulder to its wheel and allowing it to lend its shoulder to ours.

We know now that we can seek solace in the moon, that we can ask it to favor us, and perform an alchemy on our souls that makes us better, stronger, and happier. It can rid us of the things that weigh us down and give us wings to reach heights we have never dreamed of.

And so tonight, as you close your eyes, whether you have seen that night's moon or not, thank it one more time for watching over you as you sleep, as it has your every night on Earth, and that of every human who has ever been, and ever will be.

Based on the symbolism of the wheel,
Red Wheel offers books and divination decks
from a variety of traditions. We aim to provide
the ideas, information, and innovative approaches
to help you develop your own spiritual path.

Please visit our website,
WWW.REDWHEELWEISER.COM,
to learn more about our full range of titles.